My
Beloved
Sisters

My Beloved Sisters

SPENCER W. KIMBALL

Deseret Book Company
Salt Lake City, Utah
1980

Contents

A Woman's
Most
Important
Choices

My beloved sisters: There are some wonderful advantages to our modern day. There is much to be joyful about.

I come to you at this time with a message of peace and hope and love, a message of advice and counsel, a message of faith and encouragement and confidence.

May I begin by reemphasizing some everlasting truths. My dear sisters, choose to keep the commandments of God. For men, for women, for young, for old, this is the secret to happiness, here and hereafter. Keeping them with self-mastery and personal discipline allows the real freedoms that exalt and sustain us. The basic commandments are as simple as they are true: the Ten Commandments as given by God to Moses and the addition to them of what the Savior said—to love the Lord with all your heart, mind, might, and strength, and your neighbor as yourself.

Attend to your personal and family prayers and family devotions. Keep the Sabbath day holy in thought and deed. Live strictly the Word of Wisdom. Attend to all family duties. Keep your lives clean and free from all unholy and impure thoughts and actions. Cultivate those associations and activities which will not threaten and lower your high, righteous standards.

Study the scriptures. Thus you may gain strength

through the understanding of eternal things. You young women need this close relationship with the mind and will of our Eternal Father. We want our sisters as well as our men to be scholars of the scriptures. You need an acquaintanceship with God's eternal truths for your own well-being, and for the purposes of teaching your children and all others who come within your influence.

Be chaste and do everything in your power to help others to be. Be so absorbed with uplifting, enriching pursuits and pastimes that you leave no room for the negative or the evil that might move in to fill some bored or thoughtless void.

Remember always that the Lord has sanctified some things, and they are not to be forgotten or departed from. They are divine principles which, if adhered to, will make you supremely happy.

The words of all inspired prophets will teach you that violations of the law of chastity are sins in the eyes of your Heavenly Father. It is a transgression to be involved in any illicit sex activity, such as fornication or adultery. It is a transgression to become involved in lesbianism, or to engage in any lustful activity.

The sexual drives that bind men and women together as one are good and necessary. They make it possible for a couple to leave their parents and cleave unto one another. But here, more than almost any other place, we must exercise self-control. These drives, which are the fountainhead of human life, are to be allowed expression only in the sanctity of marriage.

Among your most important choices in life should be a temple marriage. Honorable, happy, and successful marriage is surely the goal of every person. One who would purposely or neglectfully avoid its serious implication is frustrating her own eternal program. Marriage is perhaps the most vital of all the decisions and has the most far-reaching effects, for it has to do not only with immediate happiness, but eternal joys as well.

In selecting one's companion for life and for eternity, certainly the most careful planning and thinking and praying and fasting should be done to be sure that of all decisions, this one is not wrong. In a true marriage there must be a union of minds as well as of hearts. Emotions must not wholly determine decisions, but the mind and the heart, strengthened by fasting and prayer and serious consideration, will give one a maximum chance of marital happiness.

Some young people think of happiness as a glamorous life of ease, luxury, and constant thrills, but true marriage is based on happiness that is more than that: the kind of happiness that comes from

9

giving, serving, sharing, sacrificing, and selflessness.

You can set your goals, young women, to make you reach and strain. Keep striving for them. Be prayerful and humble in seeking wisdom and knowledge. You are in the time of your life for studying and preparing. Learn all you can. Growth comes from setting your goals high and reaching for the stars.

Now, the General Authorities are very much aware of the fact that many of our sisters are widows. Others have become divorced. Still others have never had the privilege of temple marriage. We want all such sisters to understand that when we speak of family life, it is not done to make them feel sad or unappreciated. The leaders of the Church have said often, and clearly, that women in such circumstances include some of the most noble spirits of our Father in heaven. Those who make the best of what life has given to them will be rewarded for all that they have done in the service of our Heavenly Father and their fellowman.

Those of you who do not now experience the traditional woman's role, not by choice, but for reasons beyond control, can still do so much to help others. Your talents and time must not be misused simply because not all of the preferred ways of sharing and giving are open to you presently.

The Lord knows, too, that through circumstances beyond their control, some mothers are faced with the added responsibility of earning a living. These women have God's blessing, for he knows of their anguish and their struggle.

The Church will always hold aloft the banner of happy family life, for we can do no other. Family life is the best method for achieving happiness in this world, and it is a clear pattern given to us from the Lord about what is to be in the next world.

We have no choice, dear sisters, but to continue to hold up the ideal of the Latter-day Saint family. The fact that some do not now have the privilege of living in such a family is not reason enough to stop talking about it. We do discuss family life with sensitivity, however, realizing that many sisters do not presently have the privilege of belonging or contributing to such a family. But we cannot set aside this standard, because so many other things depend upon it.

Young women should plan and prepare for marriage and the bearing and rearing of children. It is your divine right and the avenue to the greatest and most supreme happiness. You should also make choices looking forward to the productive use of your time once the children are grown and gone from under your wing. You should seek for ways to bless the lives of all with whom you associate. You should know the truth of all things. You should be prepared to help build the kingdom of God.

You may answer that finding a husband is not within the power of a young woman. The man has the choice. To the extent that that is true, remember that what the Lord expects of each of his daughters is that she seek out those opportunities and make those choices which will keep her worthy of living again with him. Then she will be prepared for marriage.

There is a great and grand principle involved here. Just as those who do not hear the gospel in this life, but who would have received it with all their hearts had they heard it, will be given the fulness of the gospel blessings in the next world—so, too, the women of the Church who do not in this life have the privileges and blessings of a temple marriage, through no fault of their own, who would have responded if they had had an appropriate opportunity, will receive all those blessings in the world to come. We desire all you sisters to know how much we love and appreciate you. We respect you for your valiant and devoted service, and have many opportunities to observe how dedicated you are!

When I think of the women of the Church, I think of my own beloved Camilla and how greatly our family has been blessed because of her talents and leadership. What makes her—and literally millions of others who are like her—so trustworthy and so trusting? I think there are some realities we should look at.

For one thing, Mormon women are basically strong, independent, and faithful. They have chosen to live by a creed and a way of life that can be demanding at best. From the earliest days of the Church, active membership has meant faith, fortitude, denial, selflessness, and good service.

All Church programs are designed to assist us, whether we are men or women, in becoming better Latter-day Saints. All Church programs are designed to bring us closer to our Heavenly Father and to help us live lives more like that of his perfect Son, Jesus Christ.

The great women of the kingdom have often been uprooted with their husbands and families and have been moved hither and yon, yet they have not worried about God's forgetting them, because they have worshipped a God who governs the galaxies but who, in the midst of such vastness, continues to love each of his children perfectly, individually, and constantly.

Each of you should be grateful to be a woman! Self-pity is always a sad thing to see, and especially

when there is no justification for it. To be a righteous woman is a glorious thing in any age. To be a righteous woman during the winding-up scenes on this earth, before the second coming of our Savior, is an especially noble calling. The righteous woman's strength and influence today can be tenfold what it might be in more tranquil times. She has been placed here to help to enrich, to protect, and to guard the home—which is society's basic and most noble institution. Other institutions in society may falter and even fail, but the righteous woman can help to save the home, which may be the last and only sanctuary some mortals know in the midst of storm and strife.

One of the important messages that emerges from the history of great women in all ages is that they cared more for the future of their families than for their own comfort. Such good women had a grasp of what matters in life. When called upon to do so, they could fashion a lovely city in the midst of a swamp or make the desert blossom as a rose.

Selflessness is a key to happiness and effectiveness; it is precious and must be preserved as a virtue that guarantees so many other virtues. There are so many things in the world that reinforce our natural selfishness, and neither our men nor our women should be partakers thereof. We have grown strong as a people because our mothers and our women have been so selfless. That ennobling quality must not be

17

lost, even though some of the people of the world may try to persuade otherwise.

While there is much variety in the circumstances in which the women of the Church find themselves, they still have much more in common with each other than with other groups. Let us be conscious of doctrines that preach unity but that end up dividing. We hope our women as well as our men will be conscious of the philosophies of the world that would attempt to reverse the wisdom shown by the Lord when he told us that we can find ourselves only by losing ourselves.

There is a constant need to develop and to maintain tenderness. The world's ways harden us. The tenderness of our women is directly linked to the tenderness of our children. The women of the Church do so much to teach our sons and daughters and to prepare the rising generation. Let us make no mistake about it—the home is the seedbed of Saints! Both sin and selfishness destroy our spiritual sensitivity.

I am grateful for the way in which our sisters are encouraged to perform acts of Christian service as a result of their affiliation with Relief Society and other Church organizations. I hope our young women will establish early in their lives a habit of

Christian service. When we help other people with their problems, our own difficulties are put in fresh perspective. We encourage the sisters of the Church—young and older—to be anxiously engaged in quiet acts of service for friends and neighbors. Every principle of the gospel carries within itself its own witness that it is true. So it is that acts of service not only help the beneficiaries of the service, but they also enlarge the giver.

In the Sermon on the Mount, the Savior extolled, among other things, meekness, mercy, peacemaking, and the capacity to cope with persecution and misunderstanding. Women display a remarkable capacity to love and to cope, along with a remarkable empathy for others in difficulty, which moves women to service as they express their goodness quietly. Women, so often, are charity personified.

It is true of all of us that, as we progress spiritually, our sense of belonging, identity, and self-worth increases. Let us create a climate in which we encourage the sisters of the Church to have a program of personal improvement. It ought to be a practical and realistic program, one that is determined personally and not imposed upon them. Yet it ought to cause them to reach for new levels of achievement. We are not asking for something spectacular but rather for our sisters to find real self-fulfillment

20

through wise self-development in the pursuit of righteous and worthy endeavors.

We should be as concerned with the woman's capacity to communicate as we are to have her sew and preserve food. Good women are articulate as well as affectionate. One skill or one attribute need not be developed at the expense of another. Symmetry in our spiritual development is much to be desired. We are as anxious for women to be wise in the management of their time as we are for them to be wise stewards of the family's storehouse of food.

We know that women who have deep appreciation for the past will be concerned about shaping a righteous future. We desire women to develop social refinements because these are very real dimensions of keeping the second great commandment—to love one's neighbor as oneself. We know that women who will improve their relationships with our Father in heaven will also improve their relationships with their neighbors.

The women of God in all ages have been able to reflect with awe upon the handiwork of God in the heavens without neglecting the practical skills needed not only to survive on this planet but also to live an abundant life. There is more connection than many realize between the order and purpose of the

universe and the order and harmony that exist in a happy and good family.

I am grateful for the cultural refinement that comes into Latter-day Saint homes as the mothers are able to draw upon their experiences in the Church to add to the serenity of our homes. Especially is this true if they approach these things in the spirit of the thirteenth Article of Faith: "If there is anything virtuous, lovely, or of good report or praiseworthy, we seek after these things."

The cultivation of Christlike qualities is a demanding and relentless task—it is not for the seasonal worker or for those who will not stretch themselves, again and again.

Each of our sisters has the right and the responsibility to direct her own life. But be not deceived; each of us must also be responsible for our choices. This is an eternal principle. The law of the harvest is ever in evidence.

God is the same, yesterday, today, and forever, as are his purposes. It is written: "And I, God, created man in mine own image, in the image of mine Only Begotten created I him; male and female created I them." (Moses 2:27.)

And Genesis goes on to say something very beautiful about that creation: "And God blessed them. . . . And God said, Behold, I have given you . . . every thing . . . upon the earth, wherein

23

there is life, . . . and it was so. And God saw every thing that he had made, and, behold, it was very good." (Genesis 1:28-31.)

This is a partnership: God and his creation. The Primary song says, "I am a child of God." Each of us is born with a noble birthright. God is our father. He loves us. He and our mother in heaven value us beyond any measure. They gave our eternal intelligences spirit form, just as our earthly mothers and fathers have given us mortal bodies. Each of us is unique—one of a kind, made of the eternal intelligence that gives us claim upon eternal life.

Let there be no question in your mind about your value as an individual. The whole intent of the gospel plan is to provide an opportunity for you to reach your fullest potential, which is eternal progression and the possibility of godhood.

May you realize that in you is the control of your life and what you are going to be, what you are going to do. Remember that your choices may control to some extent others whose lives will be a part of your life. Remember also that if you succeed, it isn't because of luck. Success comes from faith and work and prayer and from constant righteous effort. It is a question of agency, of what you choose to do with the gifts of God—everything upon the earth wherein

25

there is life. This reverence for agency and life makes us greatly concerned about the world in which we live today. It is a world beset with evil, with frustrations, with ugliness. It makes us realize that we must make a strong stand for the right or we may not stand at all.

The Lord has never promised us that we will be free from problems and challenges. He has, however, promised that with faith we will have the strength to meet any eventuality in this life.

Being anxiously engaged in The Church of Jesus Christ of Latter-day Saints can provide for any person in any circumstance some reasons to hope—even to be glad, and certainly to be loved.

Home is a place for all that is good and enlightening and true. It should provide a climate for constant growth and learning for all who live there—father, mother, and children. Whether or not it provides such a climate depends upon each individual concerned making the right choices in life.

It is against the home and family life that Satan has aimed his greatest efforts to destroy. He strikes the moral sanctity of the home. His plan is labeled "a new morality" in which freedom of sexual relations is proclaimed. It seeks destruction of the faithfulness and fidelity of husband and wife in the face of the Lord's commandment: "Thou shalt not commit adultery." (Exodus 20:14.)

I would have each of our lovely sisters understand that there is no new morality. That the Church's stand on morality may be understood, we declare firmly and unalterably that morality is *not* an outworn garment, faded, old-fashioned, or threadbare.

As you make your life's choices, understand well that God is unchanging, and his covenants and doctrines are not susceptible to change. When the sun grows cold and the stars no longer shine, the law of chastity will still be basic in God's world and in the Lord's church. Old values are not upheld by the Church because they are old, but rather because through the ages they have proved to be right and because God has thus spoken.

The law of chastity requires total abstinence before marriage and full fidelity afterward. It is the same for both men and women. It is the cornerstone of trust so necessary to the precious happiness of the marriage relationship and family solidarity.

Satan is making yet another powerful effort to destroy the happiness and sanctity of God-ordained family life through divorce, with all its destructive forces, including heartaches, suffering, sorrow, and often disastrous results. We have often discussed the sadness and disappointments and sorrows of divorce. We can hardly emphasize it too much.

Marriage is a partnership. Each is given a part of the work of life to do. The fact that some women and men disregard their work and their opportunities does not change the program. When we speak of marriage as a partnership, let us speak of marriage as a *full* partnership. We do not want our LDS women to be *silent* partners or *limited* partners in that eternal assignment! Please be a *contributing* and *full* partner.

No matter what you read or hear, no matter what the differences of circumstances you observe in the lives of women about you, it is important to understand that the Lord holds motherhood and mothers sacred and in the highest esteem. He has entrusted to his daughters the great responsibility of bearing and nurturing children. This is the great, irreplaceable work of women. Life cannot go on if women cease to bear children. Mortal life is a privilege and a necessary step in eternal progression. Mother Eve understood that. You must also understand it.

It was never easy to bear and rear children, but easy things do not make for growth and development. Loud, blatant voices today shout, "Fewer children," and offer the pill, surgery, and even ugly abortion, which has reached monumental numbers. It is an awful thing when mothers without righteous cause take the lives or participate in the taking of the lives of their unborn children.

Much is said about the drudgery and the

confinement of the woman's role in the home. In the perspective of the gospel it is not so. There is divinity in each new life. There is challenge in creating the environment in which a child can grow and develop. There is partnership between the man and woman in building a family which can last throughout the eternities.

Mothers have a sacred role. They are partners with God, as well as with their own husbands, first in giving birth to the Lord's spirit children and then in rearing those children so they will serve the Lord and keep his commandments. Could there be a more sacred trust than to be a trustee for honorable, well-born, well-developed children? We reaffirm the Church's strong, unalterable stand against innovations or any unchastity or breaking of the laws that could possibly reflect in the lives of the children.

Of these matters I have spoken plainly because we are greatly concerned about the trends of the day that bring many serious problems and require the true daughters of God to make important choices. Never let it be said that you did not understand. Please think on these things. Pray about them, for surely I have. Prepare for and live as full a life as can be your privilege.

We thank the sisters of the Church, young and

older, for being such great defenders of the Church, in word and in deed. We love you and respect you!

As Moroni quoted to Joseph Smith from the prophet Joel, so I quote to you: "And it shall come to pass afterward, that I will pour out my spirit upon all flesh; and your sons and your *daughters* shall prophesy, your old men shall dream dreams, your young men shall see visions: And also upon the servants and upon the *handmaids* in those days will I pour out my spirit." (Joel 2:28-29. Italics added.)

May the Lord bless you and your loved ones now and always.

"Be Thou an Example"

Whenever I reflect and ponder upon the glorious truths of the gospel, and that is often, I wonder if we even begin to appreciate the implications of these wonderful truths. Let me give you a few examples.

The scriptures and the prophets have taught us clearly that God, who is perfect in his attribute of justice, is no respecter of persons. (Acts 10:34.) We know also that God is perfect in his love for each and all of us as his spirit children. When we know these truths, my sisters and associates in this divine cause, it should help us greatly as we all experience much less than perfect love and perfect justice in the world. If, in the short term, we are sometimes dealt with insensitively and thoughtlessly by others, by imperfect men and women, it may still cause us pain, but such pain and disappointment are not the whole of life. The ways of the world will not prevail, for the ways of God will triumph.

We had full equality as his spirit children. We have equality as recipients of God's perfected love for each of us. The late Elder John A. Widtsoe wrote: "The place of woman in the Church is to walk beside the man, not in front of him nor behind him. In the Church there is full equality between man and woman. The gospel, which is the only concern of the Church, was devised by the Lord for men and women alike." (*Improvement Era*, March 1942, p. 161.)

Within those great assurances, however, our roles and assignments differ. These are eternal differences, with women being given many tremendous responsibilities of motherhood and sisterhood and the men the tremendous responsibilities of fatherhood and the priesthood—but the man is not without the woman nor the woman without the man in the Lord. (1 Corinthians 11:11.) Both a righteous man and a righteous woman are a blessing to all those whom their lives touch.

Remember, in the world before we came here, faithful women were given certain assignments while faithful men were foreordained to certain priesthood tasks. While we do not now remember the particulars, this does not alter the glorious reality of what we once agreed to. We are accountable for those things which long ago were expected of us just as are those whom we sustain as prophets and apostles.

Even though the eternal roles of men and women differ, there is much to be done by way of parallel personal development—for both men and women. In this connection, I stress again the deep need each woman has to study the scriptures. We want our homes to be blessed with sister scripturians—whether you are single or married, young or old, widowed or living in a family.

Regardless of your particular circumstances, as you become more and more familiar with the truths of the scriptures, you will be more and more effective in keeping the second great commandment, to love your neighbor as yourself. Become scholars of the scriptures—not to put others down, but to lift them up. After all, who has any greater need to "treasure up" the truths of the gospel (on which they may call in their moments of need) than do women and mothers who do so much nurturing and teaching?

Seek excellence in all your righteous endeavors, and in all aspects of your lives.

Bear in mind, dear sisters, that the eternal blessings that are yours through membership in The Church of Jesus Christ of Latter-day Saints are far, far greater than any other blessings you could possibly receive.

No greater recognition can come to you in this world than to be known as a woman of God. No greater status can be conferred upon you than being a daughter of God who experiences true sisterhood, wifehood, and motherhood or other tasks that influence lives for good.

True, there are some temporary differences and some constraining circumstances. Some of our sisters have lost their husbands through death, others through divorce. Some have not yet had the great privilege of marriage. But, on the scale of eternity, the missing of these blessings shall be "but for a small moment."

Some of our sisters are experiencing the anguish that often goes with aging. Still others know the uncertainty of youth as they ponder their place in the eternal scheme of things. But real as these challenges are, each one of you needs to drink in deeply the gospel truths about the eternal nature of your individual identity and the uniqueness of your personality. You need, more and more, to feel the perfect love that our Father in heaven has for you, and to sense the value he places upon you as an individual. Ponder upon these great truths, especially in those moments when, in the stillness of such anxiety as you may experience as an individual, you might otherwise wonder and be perplexed.

Remember, too, as you focus on the glories and importance of family life here, that all of us belong to the eternal family of our Father in heaven. Be assured that all faithful sisters who, through no fault of their own, do not have the privilege during their second estate of being sealed to a worthy man will have that blessing in eternity. On occasions when you ache for the acceptance and affection that belong to family life on earth, please know that our Father in heaven is aware of your an-

guish, and that one day he will bless you beyond your capacity to express.

Sometimes to be tested and proved requires that we be temporarily deprived—but righteous women and men will one day receive *all* that our Father has. It is not only worth waiting for—it is worth living for! Meanwhile, one does not need to be married or a mother in order to keep the first and second great commandments—to love God and our fellowmen—on which, Jesus said, hang all the law and all the prophets.

Some women, because of circumstances beyond their control, must work. We understand that. We understand further that as families are raised, the talents God has given you and blessed you with can often be put to effective use in additional service to mankind. Do not, however, make the mistake of being drawn off into secondary tasks that will cause the neglect of such eternal assignments as giving birth to and rearing the spirit children of our Father in heaven. Pray carefully over all the decisions you make.

We wish you to pursue and to achieve that education, therefore, which will fit you for eternity as well as for full service in mortality. In addition to those basic and vital skills which go with homemaking, there are other skills that can be appropriately cultivated and that will increase your effectiveness in

the home, the Church, and the community.

Again, you must be wise in the choices you make, but we do not desire you to be uninformed or ineffective. You will be better mothers and wives, both in this life and in eternity, if you sharpen the skills you have been given and use the talents with which God has blessed you.

There is no greater and more glorious set of promises given to women than those which come through the gospel and the Church of Jesus Christ. Where else can you learn who you really are? Where else can you be given the necessary explanations and assurances about the nature of life? From what other source can you learn about your own uniqueness and identity? From whom else could you learn of our Heavenly Father's glorious plan of happiness?

The gospel answers are the only true answers to the questions women and men, over the centuries, have raised about themselves, about life, and about the universe. How good God has been to us all in blessing us with these answers and assurances—even though these truths place upon us serious and everlasting obligations.

How special it is for Latter-day Saint women to be given the lofty assignments they have been given

43

by our Father in heaven, especially those of you who have been privileged to be born in this part of this last dispensation. Let other women pursue heedlessly what they selfishly perceive as their interests. You can be a much-needed force for love, and truth, and righteousness on this planet. Let others selfishly pursue false values: God has given to you the tremendous tasks of nurturing families, friends, and neighbors, just as men are to provide. But *both* husband and wife are to be parents.

Finally, my dear sisters, may I suggest to you something that has not been said before or at least in quite this way. Much of the major growth that is coming to the Church in the last days will come because many of the good women of the world (in whom there is often such an inner sense of spirituality) will be drawn to the Church in large numbers. This will happen to the degree that the women of the Church reflect righteousness and articulateness in their lives and to the degree that they are seen as distinct and different—in happy ways—from the women of the world.

Among the real heroines in the world who will come into the Church are women who are more concerned with being righteous than with being selfish. These real heroines have true humility, which places a higher value on integrity than on visibility. Remember, it is as wrong to do things just to be seen of women as it is to do things to be seen of men. Great women and men are always more anxious to serve than to have dominion.

Thus it will be that the female exemplars of the Church will be a significant force in both the numerical and the spiritual growth of the Church in the last days.

No wonder the adversary strives, even now, to prevent this from happening! Regardless of who is receiving the adversary's special attention at any given time, he seeks to make all people miserable like unto himself. (2 Nephi 2:27.) Indeed, he seeks the misery of all mankind. (2 Nephi 2:18.) He is undeviating in his purposes and clever and relentless in his pursuit of them.

We love you, sisters. We have confidence in you. We rejoice in your devotion. May God bless you so that all the previous blessings promised to you will become a reality in this life and in the world to come.

I know that God lives, that Jesus is his Only Begotten Son, the Redeemer of the world, and that this is the Church of Jesus Christ, with him at its head. I leave this testimony with you, with my love and blessings, in the name of Jesus Christ.